US Congress

Julie Murray

Abdo
MY GOVERNMENT
Kids

abdopublishing.com

Published by Abdo Kids, a division of ABDO, P.O. Box 398166, Minneapolis, Minnesota 55439.
Copyright © 2018 by Abdo Consulting Group, Inc. International copyrights reserved in all countries.
No part of this book may be reproduced in any form without written permission from the publisher.
Abdo Kids Junior™ is a trademark and logo of Abdo Kids.

Printed in the United States of America, North Mankato, Minnesota.

102017

012018

THIS BOOK CONTAINS
RECYCLED MATERIALS

Photo Credits: AP Images, Getty Images, iStock, Library of Congress, Shutterstock, US Capitol, White House

Production Contributors: Teddy Borth, Jennie Forsberg, Grace Hansen

Design Contributors: Christina Doffing, Candice Keimig, Dorothy Toth

Publisher's Cataloging in Publication Data

Names: Murray, Julie, author.

Title: US Congress / by Julie Murray.

Description: Minneapolis, Minnesota : Abdo Kids, 2018. | Series: My government |
    Includes glossary, index and online resource (page 24).

Identifiers: LCCN 2017942868 | ISBN 9781532104015 (lib.bdg.) | ISBN 9781532105135 (ebook) |
    ISBN 9781532105692 (Read-to-me ebook)

Subjects: LCSH: United States--Congress--Juvenile literature. | Legislative bodies--United States--Juvenile
    literature. | Social Science--Politics & Government--Juvenile literature.

Classification: DDC 328.73--dc23

LC record available at https://lccn.loc.gov/2017942868

Table of Contents

US Congress

It was formed in 1789.

THE FIRST FEDERAL CONGRESS · 1789

5

It is made up of two parts.

They work together.

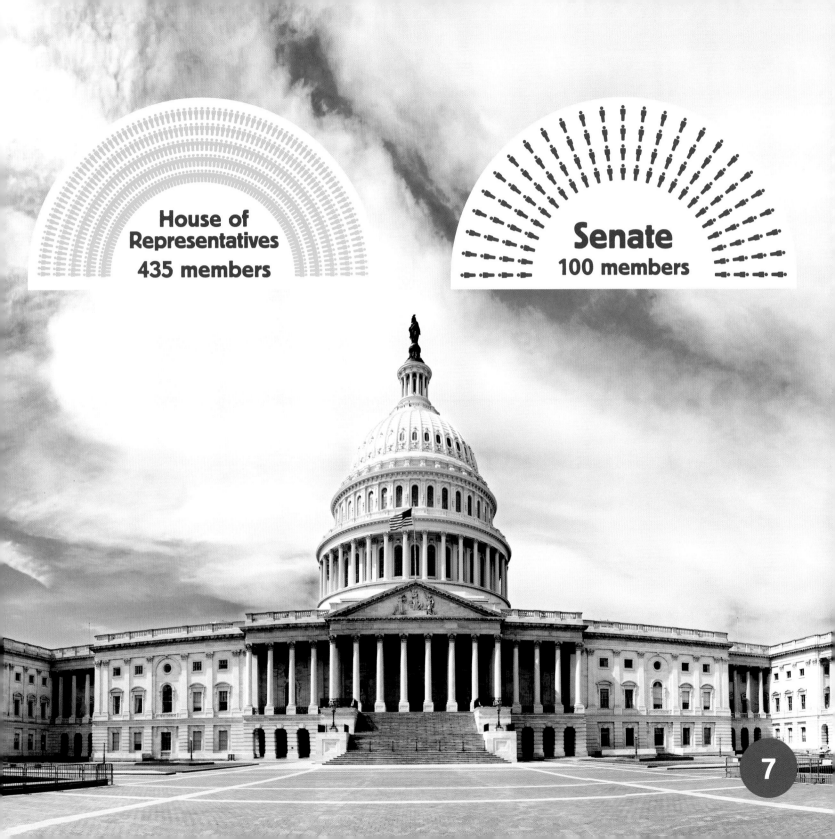

House of Representatives
435 members

Senate
100 members

7

It has 535 members.

Each one can vote.

They meet at the US Capitol.

They look at a **bill**. They vote to pass it. Now it is a law.

They can cut **taxes**. They can raise them too.

15

They can start a war.

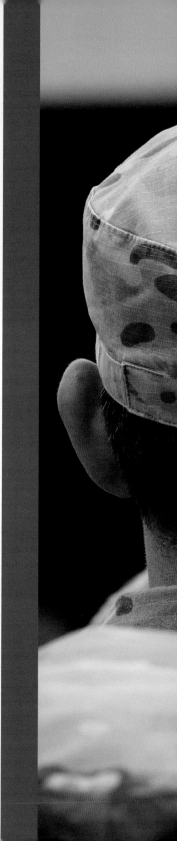

People in the US have **rights**. Congress makes sure they are kept.

19

Ava meets a senator.

What is the US Congress's Job?

decide how money is spent

declare war

make new laws

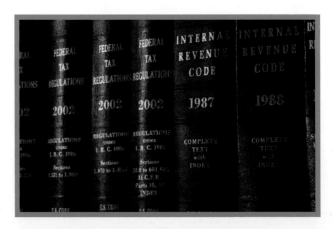

raise or lower taxes

Glossary

rights
freedoms given by the Constitution that all US citizens have that the government cannot take away.

bill
an idea for a new law that has to be passed by Congress and the president.

tax
money people pay to the government.

Index

Abdo Kids ONLINE
FREE! ONLINE MULTIMEDIA RESOURCES

Visit **abdokids.com** and use this code to access crafts, games, videos, and more!

Abdo Kids Code:
MUK4015